Surviving a Darkroom

Surviving a Darkroom
The Chronicles of Marvin Jovel McKelvey Sr.

MARVIN MCKELVEY

iUniverse, Inc.
Bloomington

SURVIVING A DARKROOM
THE CHRONICLES OF MARVIN JOVEL MCKELVEY SR.

iUniverse books may be ordered through booksellers or by contacting:

iUniverse
1663 Liberty Drive
Bloomington, IN 47403
www.iuniverse.com
1-800-Authors (1-800-288-4677)

ISBN: 978-1-4620-4960-8 (sc)
ISBN: 978-1-4620-4962-2 (hc)
ISBN: 978-1-4620-4961-5 (ebk)

Printed in the United States of America

iUniverse rev. date: 08/16/2011

Chapter 1

Life at the beginning of
my major stroke

You do not have to be in a four cornered dark room to notice you are in the dark and trying to survive. My name is Marvin McKelvey I survive a major stroke. I was only 47 at the time I had my stroke. Having a stroke took me out the world I was used to living to a whole new life. From the first day after having my stroke everything in my life from family and friends, and my job. People from all over the world, you have people with cancer, HIV and AIDS, Parkinson's disease or some just going through the recession today faces a darkroom experience in their life. Or maybe the loss of a loved one can put you in that darkroom. I always felt personally, if there were a tragic accident and my life I will want it to be fast or quick not lingering like it will be if you were hurt and disabled. I consider myself being very proud and strong before and after my stroke. Just recently there was a police officer that in the line of duty he was shot ahead and have to receive similar surgery as I did. The officer name is Anthony Diponzio. Watching his recovery, remind me a lot of what I was going through after my surgery the officer Anthony Diponzio left side was weak just like mine. I was made aware of the complications that I'll be facing after surgery. I agreed. My surgeon his name was Dr. Vates showed me my options it was a total of three options. The first one included getting to surgery and not needing to go through too many physical changes the only downside was if I elect to take that surgery that could mean my death, Dr. Vates said that could be on the operating table as well. The second one will probably paralyze my whole left side of my body only until I learned to regain my strength in using that side. The third one was just as fatal. If too much blood reaches one point to so I could have a fatal stroke. He drew me an image of two waterholes when water coming out of both ends and place in it together you have uncontrollable amount of flow of water. And that's how the blood will be on the top of my brain which will cause a surge of blood in one place and that could be just as bad as the aneurysm. The day of surgery came quickly. One week before my stroke, I started to experience weakness on my left side. My preferable vision in my left eye started to react to my stroke from the first moment my stroke began. I was unaware that a stroke was coming to view in my life. Weeks before going in the hospital to be checked on my stroke condition I was experiencing vision problems but I didn't took it seriously I just live with the problem not knowing seriousness of the condition. I might've mentioned it to certain people at work but I didn't think it wasn't that serious. Driving was difficult but I learned to deal with the situation and work around it which was the wrong thing to do. Another sign was writing home at night from work I would notice my left arm being heavy but I thought it was just from working. Being that my condition slowly creaked up on me, I learned how to make up for any loss of power and vision with my right side automatically. I was also told, that an accident that I happen to be in when I was 16 years old may have contributed to my condition. It was explained to me that when an artery such as the one that is clog had try to mend from the inside out causing a lump within the artery itself. Over the years of not eating right I develop plaque clogged each within the inside. It took a while before being totally clog but eventually it happened and I was lucky to be alive today. When I was 20 years old, I found out that I had epilepsy. No one knew at the time that it was because of the same clog that may have cause my stroke today. I was very disturbed at the age of 25 a of that I had epilepsy but with the love of Christ I was able to go forward knowing that I would have to take medication for the rest of my life because of it I was a young father and I had a job that I love and a fiancée. I had a lot of trying times understanding and dealing with seizures but I knew the only thing to do was to go forward with my life and that is what I did. My job days before my stroke was driving a forklift truck at the Xerox Corporation so I was using my arm a lot so was easy for me to think that it was from working. But I was starting to feel bad about maybe causing an accident. I never had an accident working on my forklift truck before. Every time I took a nap or sleep overnight I will wake up noticing a muscle on my left side weakening to the point I was afraid of waking up to find out that either my foot or my leg on my left side were weaker than it was before I went to sleep I was starting to get frightened because there was a change going on in my body and I couldn't explain. So I try to stay up doing something or staying busy as long as I can before long I could not keep up with myself because I needed my sleep. Two nights before I was to report to the hospital for surgery, I woke in the middle of the night to use the restroom and finding out that most of my left side was as weak as a battery going dead the artery on the right side of my neck was totally block and a lack blood flow to my brain which caused the weakening effects on my left side. That night or shall I say the next morning, I fell to the floor in my bedroom. With all the strength in me I made it to the front of my apartment and I called for an emergency van to pick me up and take me to the hospital when I got to the hospital I was scheduled for emergency surgery because my blood pressure was very high. After arriving at the hospital I called my family and friends to let them know that I was about to go to emergency surgery. The surgeon told me that I could wait to the time of surgery to make up my mind all which procedure I would like to have out of the three options that was given to me at my earlier visit. So I've picked the one that was most promising to my life to live and see my family and friends and not die on or off the operating table. Getting prepared for surgery was a very scary experience. But I remember verses from the holy Bible about I remember verses from the holy Bible on courage. The book of Deuteronomy 31:6 be strong and will encourage, do not fear nor be afraid for love thy God is with you. He would not leave you or forsake you. Joshua 1:6 be strong and of good courage, for to this people you should divide as an inheritance the land which I swore to their fathers to give to them. Phillippians 4:13 I can do all things through Christ who strengthens me. I Had nurses and techs on both sides of the bed putting needles in my arms and when they were done I had to go get half of my head shaved would've surgery would take place. Before you know it the drugs started to take effect and I was out. The surgery took 4 1/2 hours there was some complications during surgery a couple times I was told my heart stopped beating some would say I died but not too long I was able to be revised it was a difficult surgery the surgeon had to take off a small part of my skull I knew it had to be a hard thing to watch but think God they were all professionals and I lived. The operation was a success and now my biggest problem was recovering. I awoke feeling like all I did was took a nap. I Was very thirsty and hungry. When they ask me how I felt, I told them I was thirsty and hungry so I was given graham cracker and cheery Jell-O I had to be spoon fed. My favorite aunt was by my bedside along with my oldest brother and also my aunt Betty. My aunts kept telling me how much they prayed for everything to be okay and with the tears in the corner of aunt Rose's eyes made me feel loved and missed. My aunt Rose is a Christian a true believer of Christ. I am a believer also so her being there meant a lot. My mother has passed and gone to heaven five years ago so by my Rose being there gave me strength to face another day I felt so blessed just to live to see another day and little did I know it was only the beginning I'm officially in a darkroom time in my life. If you found yourself in a darkroom and a light switch was way on the other side of the room and you could see nothing in front of you not even your hand if you place it in front of your face. Before you get to the light switch there will be lots of confusion maybe you would bump into things like a coffee table chairs. Or maybe you would trip and fall over something that was plainly in front you that you cannot see because of the dark. That's no different than how I felt the day after surgery. I was confused and I didn't know what was going to happen next. When I looked to my left or right, all I could see these machines with numbers and lights on them and on my other side IV for pain. I can thank God for my life. I am a man of faith and trust and believe to my Lord Jesus Christ. I heard many stories about my victory in the operating room. The Lord is the chief surgeon of my life. The first thing I thought of after my first night. When will I be going home? Who's going to help me when I get home? Will I ever be able to move my left side again if so when. After a week past, I was on my own. Every day seems the same. I had dreams of my mother cradling me in her arms telling me everything's going to be okay. It seemed so real feelings touch and hearing her voice. I haven't seen no family no friends. Everyone seemed to go along with their life and me I had to go on with my new life which was getting better. I miss the morning meetings at work, and talking about anything but everything to my coworker. Every morning I had to learn how to set straight on the side of my bed. Every time I try to sit straight I will fall slowly to my left side. I had no balance at all. I had to learn how to brush my teeth and eat my food. I was at a disadvantage. It's hard to learn a new way of doing things from scratch like a child when you already learned them one way. I felt very embarrassed in occupational therapy because I couldn't raise my left arm just to put up blots to play certain games. It just wasn't me to have such a hard time doing the easiest thing. But I wasn't going to give up at any point. Because once you give up and do not have anything but a disabled body. One day my older and younger brother, decide to stop by right when I was going to my occupational therapy appointment. And a witness my efforts in trying to play a game with my left arm ability. And I felt so bad but little did I know there were going to be more time in my life that I have to experience that feeling of not being the old person I used to be. Living in this darkroom of my life was starting to get more confusing and difficult as they go by.

Chapter 2

Starting over my new life after stroke

Nothing never seem to stay the same from one day to the next. Out of the blue a nurse could and change your room and relocate you to another room, and if they don't change your room they would change the people who sharing a room with I've met many great people some that will be in my mind and heart forever and some that I choose to never remember. Frank was my first roommate Frank was a very nice man. Sometimes I used to joke with Frank and tell people that he reminds me of a movie that I've seen when I was young, it was a movie called the Wizard of oz. Why did Wizard of Oz? That little girl Dorothy in the picture used to always say while walking the yellow brick road, lions Tigers and Bears. When Frank snore

1 min. he sounds like a lion and the next he sounds like tigers and bears I could have a visitor at my bedside and Carl will begin to snore. That person will always jump at the sound of his snore. But we became good friends we watch the sun come up and see the sun go down. And sometimes we will pull the curtains back and watch television together. We wanted to go home so bad but we knew what was important, and that is to get better and hope that we can resume life just as we left it days later I met Ben. Ben was a nice gentleman also. If there was anything about then that I didn't like it wasn't much because we always respected each other no one wanted to be in the hospital especially in the summertime. I had to learn that no matter what goes on in the hospital, people had their life on outside of the hospital. I have one friend that would actually wheeled me in my wheelchair to the front of the hospital but when you're in a situation in life that will keep you grounded you learn a lot about people and more so yourself. Before long I had a full day activities starting with occupational and physical therapy. It seemed like a job. Having a job was one thing that I was very familiar with. I've worked for Xerox Corporation for 20 years perfect attendance, I was blessed to have such a great job and I knew it. So I held on best they can and loved it. So having discipline and procedures in my life was natural. Carl was my next roommate. Carl and I was great friends also out of all the roommates Carl was my favorite roommate because Carl needed a friend more than a roommate and I'm glad to

be that friend. There were times night Carl pain meditation didn't seem to work as good as he needed so he will bring for a nurse for more pain medicine but they were very strict and they would tell Carl you have to wait until eight o'clock or tune in next round. At that time, I believe it was more important to be Carl's friend then to keep feeding him drugs. The hospital will be very careful not to over medicate their patients so when Carl felt that he wanted more they would not give it to him. Carl had a tumor in his brain. The way his wife explains it his tumor was so large in his head that it was the size of a large grapefruit. Carl misunderstood my name and called me Harvey when he called my name. I could've corrected him but it didn't bother me because he was my friend. Sometimes Carl keep me up at night and would a low whimpering cry I would hear him call out the name he called me Havvvvvvvvey are you woke. When are they bringing the drugs for my pain? So at times, it'd just be me and Carl just lying in a hospital bed fill-in the agony of being in the hospital. Carl was a believer of God also, so one night he asked questions about Jesus Christ and I was able to answer. And also talking about life was the topic of a very long conversation and he realized that accepting Christ in his life will give him everlasting life. So that night he repeated after me "dear Lord our father, I know you died for me and rose on the third day and you're the son of God I except you in my life and please forgive me for any sin that may have committed against your name. Then time went on and we would still talk about everything and anything, because we felt that we were in a similar situation being in the hospital and all. Being that they wouldn't answer his call I would then call for him. It didn't take them long to realize that I was calling for him so they stopped answering me also. It didn't bother me much because I've never needed them for nothing but assistance to go to the bathroom. I didn't like that at all either. I felt kind of embarrassed I was used to taking care of myself all my life bearing myself that low heard of my pride but what are you going to do right. The first thing on my list was how to be more responsible for myself. The doctor told me that if I can get up out of my bed and into my wheelchair in a safe manner than they can write on the board above my bed and I do not need to call for them any longer. So that was my agenda to be trained to get in my wheelchair and that will relieve a lot of pressure from my mental state. It seemed to work good around that time because when they start ignoring Carl and my calls at night I would transfer myself in my wheelchair and I would go in the middle of the nurse station and just sit there until someone asked me why am I there, and I would tell them came the please help my friend Carl he is very uncomfortable and in a lot of pain can you see about him right now please. A while after that I became labeled as a troublemaker. I didn't think I was making trouble because Carl was my friend. Some nights when he couldn't sleep it a keep me up at night so I would transfer myself in my wheelchair and wheel my chair over to his bedside and we would talk about anything until he gets sleepy. Carl believe in God, so I will talk to him and try to comfort him and tell him about Carl was very happy that his name was written in the book of eternal life. And I will stay there and hold his hand and the fear in his heart will fade away." In the holy Bible the book of Isaiah 41:10 for I am with you ; be not dismayed, for I am your God. I will strengthen you, yes, I will help you, I will uphold you with my righteous right hand. And if I haven't gotten to know him I would've never known that Carl was a farmer. Carl had goats, and cows, horses and dogs. I told him when I get better I would love to visit and learn more about his life. Before long Carl was home and I was still there. It almost felt as if I was in a jail or being incarcerated because I couldn't do anything but just laid there. But it was a long before I transferred myself in my wheelchair sign myself up and went to the front of the hospital and enjoyed outside all by myself it wasn't permitted, but I've done it anyways, especially when the sunny and cloudy days between visits from family and friends. That's just the kind of person I am couldn't sit me still for nothing. I've made the Dean's list and work full-time for Xerox. As Xerox Corporation worker, I've worked 40 to 52 hours a week and still manage to stay on the Dean's list at college. I believe I've gotten that kind of strength from my mother. No matter what kind of hurdle set before my mother she always manage to put 1 foot in front of the other and with all six of her kids, my three brothers and three sisters my mother with no help at all will give everyone enough love and strength to go forward. It seemed like growing up from five years old up to junior high school we moved our home once a year but everyone was happy because we had our mother. My mother my father was divorce, and I did not hear from my father as often as I like but when it comes to loving someone my mother wrote the book I know right now if she was alive she would probably tell me that if she can she would give me her legs. That was the kind of mother she was. One night I had a dream about my mother, that I was a infant child and I was in her arms and I could see her hand rubbing my leg and comforting me telling me that it's going to be okay. That was the kind of mother that I had.

Chapter 3

Over a year has passed
time to get started

Time has passed every morning by doctors will all meet in my room for my morning examination after my surgery and I ask over and over again visit after visit when am I going home. But they will always say maybe tomorrow. I think after a while from the looks on their face they were starting to get pretty annoyed but I kept asking when am I going, going home today? Till one day at my surprise my doctor said if I have good news and bad news. Good news is was to keep improving it would be sooner than I think. The bad news is your apartment has too many stairs so you have to look for a different place to the home to maybe family. But I was getting set against that I want to go to my house A social worker visit me one morning and gave me a list of housing move into that will be set for people disabled. Like for wheelchairs handicap parking and other necessities for disabled. There was no way I was going to uproot my home and move in a neighborhood that I never seen before nor people that I don't know. But this is where faith, come in to my life, Hebrews 11:1 now faith is the substance of things hoped for, the evidence of things not seen. And I knew that the Lord words were true, and I have faith that I will see home again. I never knew the time I went to the hospital or surgery that I would not see my living room again. So I was set inside my head to go home and I knew that I will see home again. The next morning my doctor see how bad I wanted to go to my home she instructed me to write a list of people who support me in times of need if needed with phone numbers so they can be reached and if that is completed by the next week I can go home. I didn't have that many people to choose from at that time because it seemed like everyone start to visit less in some ways care less. But I've learned not to hold anything against anyone at this point of my life. So my mind starts wandering and I started digging to find the answer to go home again. Little did I expect my son stepped up to the plate and said he would live with me half a day and work the other half if that help me go home. It felt like I was being release from a confinement of some sort. But little did I know the fight had only just begun in my life to live again. Having small but comfortable income at that time helped a lot to get my life started. But quickly I learned that people will be right by your side when you have money but after while like I was told from a friend in the hospital lots of times they seem to disappear. I would've never known how true his advice was until I experience it myself. I've had one friend that was very dear to me she seemed to really take care of herself at that time but slowly her life was going down the drain because of drugs but I could see nor understand at that time. I help purchase her car to help if I needed her but month after getting home the car had to be junked, that was my first mistake. I also prayed about the situation and I felt that by her being ungodly it was insulting my spirit of Jesus because I give a lot of credit of the existing today to my Lord Jesus Christ and I didn't think that she was responsible for a lot of success of me being here. I want to give the Lord the credit of a lot of my success first my life and survive the surgery, second being home third for me to be able to cope at home. I figured if I learn to deal with the steps that I had at my home if I successfully go through the trials of having them in my life you only make me stronger form of future life and possibly get well sooner. It was such a task to handle. I had occupational and physical therapy at my house for a little while as long as my insurance would carry. Months later I had to learn how to take care of myself by myself because one day a time will come and no one will be there so to prevent the heartbreak and depression I must be a successful as I was before my stroke. I found it very hard to do but I wasn't going to quit. Besides what else can I do but accept my situation and pray that one day I will be happy as before my stroke. Thank God I had a mother, with so much strength, and so much fight to pull me through a lot of hard times. But it was the knowledge of God and his son Jesus Christ that gave me the focus that I need to be happy. This dark room was starting to get shades of light in my life. I remember waking up one morning in the hospital not knowing what's coming next and feeling that my life was stolen from me and wondering if I would ever see it again or day of being home in my house sitting on my couch cooking my own food and sleeping peacefully in my own surroundings and not in a hospital. You can see what I mean about surviving the dark room, the dark room was definitely confusing scary at times and lonely. Every day carried a new hurdle I was not one of let nothing stop me from taking it one day at a time and doing the best I can when you look at the overall picture that's what's fun and make sense out the whole ordeal. Another lesson learned at that time was the fact that some people would say things to make themselves feel better and appreciated and hold it high above your needs like example I'll call you later and see how you doing or you're doing great looks fine maybe someday out, watched the game with you or maybe go to the park. Little did I know that it only made them feel better thinking that they are making me feel better but in all actuality it was to make them feel better because of guilt that they may feel at that time because they would never follow through with whatever they may suggest thinking they were making me feel better. I had a frightening dream, this dream actually was put a fear in my heart, hoping it will never come true, that fear was the people that either relied on were gone. I've really learned a lot in them days of my life. I must thank God for giving me the knowledge of what I've learned. Depending on people don't feel good to me because I was so use to depending on myself for a very long time. I've grown to find out sometimes in life, you may need someone to be there to help you. I never thought that a day will come and I would actually be in need of someone help.

Chapter 4

Not letting fear guide my life

After being home for some months fear always been the corner of my mind, am I going to fall down stairs, falling while cooking, what is I had no one to turn to if I was in trouble, how long am I going to be able to go this way. There is always fear in the back of my mind so I kept in mind what God said that was FEAR NOT for I am with you; be not dismayed, for I am your God. I will strengthen you, yes, I will help you, I will uphold you with my righteous right hand. Isaiah 41: 10(KJv) and my favorite verse from the Bible second Timothy chapter 1 verse seven full God has not given us a spirit of fear and timidity, but of power, love, and self discipline. That invoice which is Holy Spirit save me a lot of ways to go forward. With God to my side and nothing could stop me from going forward. There was a great fear in my heart when it came to driving because of my left peripheral vision. In the holy Bible second Timothy chapter 1 verse seven, for God has not given us a spirit of fear but of power, love and self discipline. Many faces of fear one is doubt and another's unbelief. Worry is fear based fear not come from God. Fear and faith operates on the same laws. There is something call the law of reciprocal. If you look at a compass, you have North and South they are direct opposites. Faith comes by hearing the word of God, fear is a contradiction of the Word of God. If you want to see God operate in your life you must have faith, and when fear is operating your life can you not operating your life and faith. Fear is just contaminated faith. Fear tolerated is faith contaminated. If you put up with fear in your life at any level it will contaminate your faith. When you allow faith in your life you allow God to operate in your life. I was told by my occupational and physical therapy and my social worker from the hospital that I was not permitted to drive my car yet. One day I came home to find a note under my door and said BUSTED it was a note by my physical therapist letting me know that she was there while I was not. It was funny in a way because she knew where my car is usually park. I guess you could say I was fearless but I must say I was scared. I will not allow fear to operate in my life. Driving to me felt as if I was behind the wheel for the very first time. It wasn't me that I was afraid of, it was the other drivers that will be around me they can be behind me on either side. It was just a thought of being hit by another car. That was fear disguising itself as wary. I was very determined to have God in my life in every way possible I wasn't going to let fear rule my life besides that I have God on my side. Greater is he that is in me that's in this world. Things didn't always go as smooth as I would like it to go but I managed. One day at a time. One Day my car was broadsided by another car while I was on my way home from the market. My car came close to being total, so at that moment the clouds were over my head and I felt so bad that all I can do is pray. It hurt me so that no one else like a innocent bystander was hurt and that scene. Someone could've been walking on the sidewalk at that time and gotten hurt. My spirits were lifted once again feeling the present of God in my life. Once again I Went to spirit the Lord, for me and told me to go upstairs in my apartment sit down learn more about him and have an intimate relationship with him and he will take care of everything outside my door and I shall take care knowing him and worshiping him. Being close to God was the biggest guidance of getting out that darkroom that I once lived in when I have my stroke. Weeks later my car was home in shape freshly painted and ready for the next plans to make it a perfect car. Yes, it was only a car but it was mine and all paid for. My faith in God has grown so large at that time. While I was in my home watching television I notice a story about a man who lost one of his legs and he was hoping and wishing to have an artificial leg attached to his body. All I could say is that I am very blessed because I have a leg already attached to my body and I can feel with that Leg something he would never ever have so I am very blessed to be alive and have legs on my body if that not blessed I couldn't say you what blessed is. The Lord help me with my life and my dreams. Little time has passed and I wanted to do some work on my engine on my car so I took it to the dealership and found out that my engine was cracked which may model car priceless. While waiting on the keys to take my car home a mechanic delivered the news that he couldn't find my keys to my car I couldn't figure out anything at that point so I pray and I ask God to take me out of this mess that I was in, moments later another guy walked in the room and offered me another car same make and model let younger year for half the price of the original, and even added a sunroof on the car. If that not the love of Christ I couldn't tell you what. The Lord is the biggest thing in everyone's life. If tragic or horrific things subject your life the Lord will step in your life and take over a situation for your good, it's the Lord's will to bring people closer to God and that should be people concern also. It has nothing to do with magic or luck. In this journey in my life today I knew that everything in my past did not mean what I thought it did, I am now ready to go forward, I might not have all the answers but I have an ideal. Faith and fear are opposites if you trade one over the other in the first don't exist. Each trial in my life was proven by faith in each trial in my life was a burden would fear. It's my belief that when the Lord calls one door he opens other doors in your life and between the doors there's a hallway and that hallway can be a bunch of trials and tribulations some would say hellish things that can invade to life. The spirit of God pressed on my heart very heavily in the days gone by. I felt the need to forgive anyone that I felt had done me wrong. The Bible says Matthews 6:14 for if you forgive men their trespasses, your heavenly father will also forgive you. John 1:9 if we confess our sins, he is faithful and just to forgive us our sins and to cleanse us from all unrighteousness Mark 3:29 but he who blasphmes against the Holy Spirit never has forgiveness but is subject to eternal combination. Romans 4:7 bless are those whose lawless deeds are forgiven, and whose sins are covered; Ephesians 4:32 and be kind to one another, tender hearted forgiving one another, even as God in Christ forgave you. At times giving yourself is your first step.

Chapter 5

Bitterness and anger start to set in my life

Growing up I never considered myself as an angry person. But after everything I went through from the very beginning there were always obstacles to cross starting with not having visitors while I was in the hospital. Being bitter and angry, and lonely, and hurting, was experiences that develop a lot. Once the bitterness set in then you get angry. Getting home finally made things very great, but not long after the bitterness set in all over again because I didn't have too many visitors all over again. The holy Bible says Proverbs 14:17 a quick man at foolishly, and a man of wicked intentions is hated. Poverbs 14:29 **he** was slow to wrath has great understanding but he that is impulsive exalts folly. Proverbs 16:32 he who is slow to anger is better than the Might, and he who rules the spirit than he who takes the city. Psalms 37:8 cease from anger, and forsake wrath ; do not fret it only causes harm. Ephesians 4:26 be angry, and do not sin; do not let the sun go down on your wrath let all bitterness wrath anger clamor and evil speaking, be put away from you be put away from you, let all malice. James 1:19-20 so then my beloved brother, the everyman be swift to hear, slow to speak, slow to wrath for raffles man does not produce the righteousness of God. Psalms 19:105 your word is a lamp to my feet and a light to my path. The kind of bitterness and anger was the same kind I experience when I was in the hospital. The dark room started to set in all over again in my life. But one way of fighting anger and bitterness was to worship God in all his goodness. Worshiping God not a hard thing to do. I praise the Lord that's another way of thinking him. Chronicles 29:13 now therefore, our God, we thank you and praise you glorious name I will praise the Lord according to his righteousness. Psalms 7:17 I will praise the Lord according to his righteousness, and will sing praise to the name of the Lord most high. Psalms 51:15 oh Lord, open my lips, and my mouth shall show forth your praise. Psalms67:3 let all the People praise you, Psalms 106:1 praise the Lord,oh give thanks to the Lord for he is good, for his mercy endures forever. Praise the Lord, Lord God Listening to worship song on the radio or just thinking him for good things that you have been blessed with. But you also need to thank him for that thing that you going through. When you going through bad times and you don't have an answer and you pray for a answer and you don't seem to get it that doesn't mean that God did not hear you or possibly answered prayer. Sometimes the answer we want doesn't feel good or maybe the answer doesn't come on we want it. Going through the struggles of my stroke, I prayed many a time in the Lord answered me. But instead of allowing me to go through the same mess that I went through, the Lord had a way of showing me my mistakes and would love and forgiveness the Lord correct me and gave me a new way. And if the Lord did not show me my mistakes I would of still be doing the same thing that got me in the position that I'm in today. Not only that I would know have the pleasure of being a blessing to others. I wasn't going to quit. It's funny to see people come into your life and disappear or maybe I shouldn't say funny but that's what was starting to happen. I start to learn a lot about people that I knew. It seemed that they had their own agenda in your life. It was my belief that some people actually need to hear themselves as being someone there really not when they say something good thinking that the cheering you up, by telling you things and not backing it up. It seemed as if it made them complete to make you think that they are nice or generous with their feelings when all along whatever they say doesn't turn out the way that they say it will. But I learned how to forgive them when it happened. Most of the time people only want you to be happy. I found it very hard to understand that for a long time. It's a very dark room that I was living in having a stroke. It was my wish that they wouldn't say things they really don't mean especially when they give you their word and don't back it up because giving your word is like a signature and it should mean exactly what they said. It hurts more when they turn out to be not truthful to their word. I feel that a person word is very final invaluable. A person is only as good as their word. There was a man I met at physical therapy one day and he told me that he didn't feel as good as he would like to feel even though he was in a wheelchair he still had great spirits it was only the fact that ever since he was in a wheelchair he watched the people of his life one by one starting to disappear. I was starting to understand exactly what he was saying. I didn't then but I do now. I can only imagine the hurt and pain he was going through at that time. I didn't then but I do now and he was so right. I had a great childhood with a loving parent, my mother. My father was living but I didn't see much of my father growing up. Going back to when I was five years old I remember how hard it was for my mother raising me and my three brothers and three sisters. I never seen my mother in tears but I always felt that the fight in her because raising children on your own can hold a lot of triumphs and disappointments. I say Disappointments because she always wanted the best for her children. It seemed like we moved to a new home every other year. So our surroundings changed a lot. We will be going through life happy and satisfied and then out of nowhere my mother will call us together to tell us we're moving again. The reasons why always been because of affording our home that we rent or some kind of landlord dispute. It could've been because of condition or some kind of grown up reason that we really never understood being kids. My mother will find a home and by herself she will organize a safe moving possibility for all of us. I have three brothers and three sisters and I love my brothers and sisters. And when the time came for dinner my mother always had a plan to make sure her kids come first. She made sure we had three meals a day and how she managed that is still very puzzling to me because we started out on public assistance. My mother used to be surviving the dark room as long as I can remember. She would be in her bedroom sitting on the side of her bed trying to find a way for all of us to be happy. My mother always worried about how things were going to turn out. But she successfully pulled it off every time. Growing up me and my sister Rita didn't think they were anything my mother couldn't do. In some ways we thought she were God because we had so much love given to us that if she was gone for a day we will worry about our tomorrows. Growing up I could sense she did not know all the answers but she would not give up until everyone's happy. That is why surviving my dark rooms in my life today I have a great reference in my past and that is my loving mother. Days before she passed away she was in tears in her hospital bed and I've asked her what was wrong and she told me that she was not afraid of dying she was just sad because she wanted to do so much for children and she will not have a chance to because she was dying. So wiping the tears from her eyes I tried to ensure her that everything was going to be okay and she was the greatest mother in the world. I find myself today sitting on the side of my bed in heavy thought about my tomorrow just like her. And God has given me the greatest thoughts on struggling through my problems by giving me my mother. One day I woke up and praying like every morning I ask God where is my help and in my spirit deep down in my heart I heard a answer and answer was that I was given a wonderful mother who influenced me in every way today. When it comes to surviving a darkroom my mother is number one in my book because not only did she raise seven children at one time by herself she also allow my grandmother to leave the hospital and live with us because she need care. Back when I was in a second grade I was going to elementary school in the city of Rochester New York, and I had a little friend same age as me tell me that he was going home to play catch with his dad, and it hurt me so bad. The reason why me and my friend got into a fight that day was I told him that dad's are not supposed to live with you only mother's raise you so we fought over who was right. I ran home straight to my mother and I told her why I've got into a fight and she told me that he was right and I was wrong I was even more puzzled but she wiped my tears and love me for more and that is why she is so special to all of my brothers and sisters including myself. My mother loved me so much that I did not find out that I only have one life until I was in a third-grade. It was funny in a way I found out because I was in a classroom with 10 other children my age and the teacher will write a picture on the board and have each child use their imagination and in the story that she wrote on the board. And when he got to be my turn looking at the illustration the story end with a man dying more than once and to my surprise I found out that you only live once. And the reason I never really knew about death was because of the love that surrounded me in my home. I never really seen my mother angry for no reason at all she always manage to do the right thing at the right time to protect her children. I believe I've gotten my strength today from that sweet lady. My mother died January 2, 2002 I'll never forget that day. I'm so glad that I've had a chance to show her how much I love her before that day came. I'm so glad that she did not live to see the day I suffered because it would've hurt her so much. When I was 22 years old I was diagnosed with epilepsy and when I opened up my eyes for first-time after being in the hospital she was right by my bedside. She loved every child of hers equally she was a very special lady. One problem that really bothered her a lot was not seeing her brothers and sisters. I go through the same thing today so I know the pain that she went through first-hand and I understand more of my past that I never knew today. The only difference I see is that I never seen my mother bitter or angry. I guess that is one expression my mother never wanted us to see. And that's why I know for fact that you do not have to live your life angry bitter upset or worried. You never know when life deals you a bad hand all you can do is pray to God learn more about your reasons for being on this earth and worshiping Jesus for allowing you to have your days on earth. If it wasn't for the death of Jesus we would not be here today. So one of your reasons for being here today is to worship God and thank God for allowing his son to die for our sins. It is easy to think everything happens by chance but that is so wrong because God knows why you're here even knows every hair that is on your head. It should never be took for granted how big God is in everyone's life. Some people say things like how could God allow such a bad thing to happen to them or someone that they love but it's not about them or the person they love it's about God and his kingdom. It doesn't matter what religion you believe it it's only one God and he should be loved by everyone. Like the commandment says we shall love our God and put no other God before him. Everyone experience God's love in their life. It is never God's intention for anyone to hurt in their life. Sometimes the things we go through is more than what we see, it's our faith in God that what we lack to understand. When I go to a store to shop and people see how much I love Jesus, they know that there's another way around their pain and that's not through certain people that's on this earth but through the love of God. It gets hard at times but keeping my faith pulls me through the hard times. It's the blood of Jesus that heals us and save us through tormented times. If it wasn't for the blood of Jesus dying on the cross for our sin we would not be living today. And if you wonder why they're going through dark rooms of our lives have any good then we need to think about others that's in our life. If you were in a darkroom situation in your life, and someone was in a similar situation, would you want to help them get out the darkroom along with yourself? Well that's how I feel, I don't expect everyone to feel the way I feel, but it's only natural not to see another person suffered. When I accepted Jesus in my life, I asked Jesus to use me in any way possible to bring God's will in my life and the lives around me. So allowing God to use me on this earth, God uses my situation to better me and the people that I may run into with in my path see him and worship him as the one and only God he is. You may not feel good a time but I have faith that whatever I'm going through he's there that that builds my character strengths, and faith in my situation. The only way I can make it through my days of being in the darkrooms of my life is with Jesus. The holy Bible is an open book that must be read by everyone because the answers are all in the book. When you experiencing a darkroom in your life Jesus is there, when you confuse or heart, Jesus forgiveness is there. You're never alone in that darkroom. In real life if you are surrounded by four walls and a dark and alone, you want someone to be with you and hold your hand will Jesus will hold your hand and walk with you talk with you take your fear away and fulfilled your heart and give you directions on how to get out of your darkroom. I know because he's with me. And even though things do not come easy in my life I have Jesus. Jesus would never leave you or forsake you. I know firsthand how great that feels to have a friend or someone to hold your hand in times of fear and loneliness. It doesn't matter what your problem may be the Lord is there with his arms open and ready to receive you back home. It's like the prodigal son and the holy Bible, Jesus tells the story of a man that took his inheritance and left home and thinking that he was going to be happy this man spot on his inheritance on wishful things to had nothing. One day that man had nowhere to go and no more money to spend any come to realize that home is where he should be. When he finally came to his senses he went home and his father opened up his arms and greeted his son with love and compassion as if he never left his home. Well we all are prodigal son and daughters of the Lord and he standing back with his arms wide open welcoming us home with the same kind of love and all we must do is receive the Lords gift of forgiveness. All we must do this except his gift. No one has to work for this gift all we must do is receive, and no by faith that Jesus Christ is the son of God and Jesus died on the cross for our sins and rose on the third day.

Chapter 6

It all comes down to survival

There is a saying from people that you may be in the Army and that is if you win the battle you win the war. Life today we fight many battles in our life. The battles may also be darkroom that we must survive from. Our battles are already won by Jesus dying on the cross. My battle was my past stroke. Every day I live I live in victory. The battles in your life can be physical or emotional your way you must fight and if you fight you may win. In the holy Bible there is a verse you must keep in mind. First Timothy chapter 6 verse 12 reads, fight the good fight of faith, lay hold on eternal life, whereunto thou are also called and hast professed a good profession before witnesses. My battle dealing with my stroke I have won. Having Christ in

my life and believing that he had died on the cross for my sins
I believe that Christ walks with me and all my battle in my life.
There is one more thing that a believer must keep in mind and
that is the Holy Ghost or some may say the Holy Spirit. Having
the Holy Spirit in your life also means being anointed. Being
anointed is allowing God to guide you through your struggles
and your problems. Success in your faith may consist of being
anointed. Being anointed, you win every battle on the time.
Battles are real to life but victory is more real to the believers
of Christ Jesus. I believe that Christ Jesus the son of God died
on the cross for my sins. Having annoying in my life makes me
wonder sometimes, how did I do that? How did I make it to that
difficult surgery? How am I walking today after being paralyze?
How is the support of the anointing in my life so strong that I
didn't need people around me at certain times of my recovery?
You cannot have the anointing without the annoying one. So
if you fail to not have the annoying one in your life then my
advice is to get the Anointing one in your life, and that's having
Christ. If you're wondering how to do that well all you have to
do is confess that Jesus Christ died on the cross for your sins
and rose on the third day, and I ask the Lord to live in your
life and to guide you. It is that simple. God is a forgiving God
he will not turn you away no matter what you have done and
you pass. There is nothing too bad or unforgiving to father
God. There is going to be battles that you are not going to win
in your natural abilities. You are going to need help and that

is Holy spirit. There are people today that I hate that word anointing spirit or the Holy Ghost. I can say we all know that battles are real and I life today. I've learned firsthand how a battle in life can make you feel alone lonely and in despair and sometimes pain and when I realize that I could've been dead and have died on the operating table while the surgeon was repairing my blocked artery on the right side of my brain what bigger battle can be won then life. I accepted Jesus in my life and in my heart and turned my life over to Jesus the son of God. It is also written in the holy Bible second Corinthians chapter 2 verse 14 reads, now thanks be unto God which always causes us to triumph in Christ and maketh manifestthe savour of his of his knowledge by us in every place. So like it is first mentioned thanks be unto God, we must learn to thank God every chance we get an iLife. Just like it has been written thanks be unto God that I survive my surgery, thanks be unto God that I am home in my own house taking care of myself. Thanks be unto God that I had a good day, thanks be unto God that I have food to eat today. Thanks be unto God that I have the Holy Spirit guiding me and helping me along my way to being 100% healed in my life. Hallelujah Thanksgiving to God is not just thinking God for things that has been manifested in your life. It is also for things that you would like to see manifest in your life and faith. You may seem as if you're in a desert with nothing to hold onto no hope in sight but thinking God will bring you through. You may seem to think you in the middle of chaos but thinking God will get you through any situation in your life I'm a living witness to that fact. Will always causes us to make it through all situations in our Life and that includes surviving are darkroom in our lives. Christ is not Jesus was last name. He did not say which always causes us to make it to Jesus Christ literally means the anointing or the anointed one and his anointing our victories are only promise through the anointing it's not guarantee outside the anointing so you can be a Christian and not experience victory if you're not in the anointing. Thanks be unto God who causes us to make it through the anointing one in his anointed when you wake up in the morning is the right thing to do is pray to Jesus and to develop a intimate relationship with Jesus and the anointed. The anointing and anointed one Jesus Christ is his real as the trees or the stars you see in the sky and having an intimate relationship will bring you comfort to every situation in your life. So while you're trying to make it out of that darkroom in your life you should know that you're never alone the anointed one is always with you and always hear your cries. Two worlds naked I it looks as if you're by yourself but you never alone.

Chapter 7

Being content and determine to move forward or getting out of your situation

When I finally made it home from the hospital, a lot of things in my life felt very impossible to follow through without the help of others. But the one thing that really bothered me that was calling on others for something as little as sitting and talking and sharing time some little as watching television or just being good company. When the time came for me to have that company in my life it was for something like going to the grocery store or maybe help in cleaning my home. So I would sit down and have a conversation with the Lord. Sitting and talking to the Lord strength my intimate relationship with the Lord. After thanking him for being so important in my life, and praising him for all the goodness around me, I would tell the Lord about my day and what's bothering me. The pressures in life seem to come in groups. It seemed as if everything cost money. But I did not hesitate paying my way for help in my life. Over time I was able to notice when people care more about the money than helping me with my needs. When people seem to care more about money than my needs I quickly remember how I used to be able to take care of myself. For example, if I needed to go to the grocery store for little needs like deodorant dishwashing liquid or something like an electronic need like a fan or computer needs CDs maybe a new television. Over time I became more content to do it myself. Not because of the money but because of my past living. I lived on my own all my life and I did not have any problems doing all the things that I needed to do. While shopping I felt as if I was handicap. I have met a lot of disabled and handicapped people along the way and they were very nice people. I have nothing against handicap or disable individuals but my pride was very hard to deal with coming home. Many times after waking up in the morning I noticed the difference between what I used to could do and what I can't do today. At times it felt relaxing dreaming because in my dreams I did not have the same problem that I have today. But I was going to keep trying to do the best I can at everything that I approach in my life from going down two flights of stairs to doing my own shopping. I prayed if not twice three times a day that one day the problems that I face will be thing of the past. But the more I prayed and asked God to make me well I learned how to believe that one day it happened, and that there is a reason for everything. One day I realized that a lot of the things that surround me today were things of yesterday. My past living is what got me in the situation today. I was determined to change my future because I could not change my past. Thank God that I have a memory to take me back and see all the things that I knew that wasn't right and my life and did not make any advances to change. Starting now I'm going to make a difference in my life and the lives around me. That was a very difficult thing to do. Not long ago I was a songwriter of R&B records and I influence other people through my music and a godless lifestyle. I've owned hundreds of R&B recording on CD, and I was very determined to do things right in my life going forward. I made up my mind that in one way or another I want to influence people in a better way and that's telling people about my Jesus and the difference worshiping Jesus in my life change me into a better person. Remembering back in church my pastor preach to the whole conjugation about how certain things that does not contain the work of Christ in your life might be something to hold you back from the blessings in your life. He also mentioned about the struggle it would be for anyone to take authority of their own life to live a sinless holy way of living with things holding you back. Back when I used to attend my old church my pastor, Pastor Reginald McGill show me how to be humble in my life. There were times after a long service I used to go to

Pastor McGill and I used to be so eager to talk to him about a dream or something that was bothering me and he will always ask me did I pray about it and what did Jesus say. Back then I kind of felt that I was being ignored but he was so right in his teaching back then I had so much to learn I'm just very blessed that I had such a good teacher. I really think Pastor McGill for helping me develop a foundation to build on. One thing and that foundation that I built was not allowing things in my past to have an effect on my future. I've gotten rid of all of my old CDs except my jazz CDs and from that day forward I concentrated on friends and people with things that do not influence and holy life or living. That's how determine I was to straightening up my life. I was very content to moving forward and everything I do. I did not have to worry much about the people because they seem to drop off on their own. As depress as it made me, I feel that it also was a blessing. With every person that left my life God replaced them with beautiful people that I could count on. It was awkward at first but I've learned how to deal with the situation. Some people I seem right away and my past were really going down the wrong road in their life, and I knew right away that they cannot be a part of my future because if they grieve the Holy Spirit in my life they grieve me too rather I want to believe it or not I know what is right. While walking through places like the store or Dr. appointments I could feel eyes looking at me because my walking was still kind of funny. I still had to regain a lot of strength in my left leg and I had a brace on the lower part of my leg but I did not let that bother me. Some people were still kind of rude like in the grocery store pushing carts but then there were lots of others who were gentle and nice and always had great comments, you can say they were very warm hearted. Even though it was a struggle I still push forward. I figured I'm going to my heart and everything I do. If I had a choice I would get on a plane and go to many different places, like conferences, and historical events. One day my dreams will come true because I believe in God and I have God's faith. With God in my life I do not believe he is brought me this far to leave me. What makes a good saint is a saint that gets back up when he falls down. I have learned by going to church on a regular basis that the Lord our God do not make any mistakes. We are not inflicted with more pain than we can bear in our lives. The Lord knows everyone that lives on this earth. The Lord knows every hair that is on our head. Sometimes the problems we face in our live are really good for steppingstone into glory. It is all good for his glory on earth. And knowing that, I try to make my experiences that I'm facing work for the Lord's good as well as my own. Getting in touch with my spiritual life has help me to deal with my disabilities from my stroke. I mean being content and determine gives others hope and strength. There is in a day that goes by that I want to cry in defeat. I don't let defeat be a part of my life. I serve a God that is more than capable of healing my physical and mental needs. If I have to give up everything in my life I will believe in my God to help me through. When I wake in the morning I think God for giving me the spirit and love to help me follow through. When I lay down at night I can be so exhausted and my feelings can be so hurt but I remember that the God I serve loves me enough to allow his only son to die for me on the cross and that is more love than any human that I know can ever do. There are people who faces many difficulties like I do in life and I am proud to give others encouragement to live and do the best they can because with the Lord in our lives we would never be alone. That is one thing that stays in my mind. If the Lord was to come to my house I will have a place for him and love because he loved me first. We hear about tragedies everyday that goes on around us I will pray for tragedies that the people involved will someday know him as well as I do. Many of times I would take my last and give it to someone in need and every time the Lord will replace whatever loss that I might encounter. Second Corinthians 9:7 let each one give as he purposes in his heart, not grudgingly or necessity, for God loves a cheerful giver. Psalms 41:1 to the chief musician, a Psalm of David blessed of he who considers the poor, the Lord will deliver him in times of trouble. Proverbs 19:17 he who has pity on the poor lends to the Lord and he will pay back what is given. Peter 1:5 but also for this very reason, giving all diligence, add to your faith virtue to virtue knowledge. It's about having faith that he's there and will never leave me. We all have some kind of dark room to live through. If we don't see it now, we will see it one day of our life. When it comes down to being determined, I am very determined to live life in eternity because that is what the Lord promised to anyone who accept and welcome Jesus Christ into their life and pray to God to come into their life and acknowledgment that his son Jesus Christ has died for their sins. So there is nothing anyone can go through that can give you a better outcome or promise. I count it all joy to live for Jesus Christ.

Chapter 8

Learning truths light and recovery from the dark

The truth is I had a stroke. I must learn to accept what has happened to my body and the surgery which left my skull with a hole from the surgery. The light is I'm determined to get well and live a long life. Jesus said what's in the dark soon come to light I found that light when I accepted Jesus to help me through my problems. Surviving a darkroom is very true for many events and people live. If you don't learn how to accept going forward can be a very difficult thing to do. During this time you must learn the things of your heart. And in the holy Bible, when Moses was chosen to lead people out of Egypt he took his darkness and he learned how to accept his future. It wasn't all roses for Moses and that time. Even though he was labeled as a killer he still had to learn when he learned the light was shown he followed the truth and he accepted who and what he was and through all his difficulties he pressed forward. One of Moses found it difficult because he could not speak clearly, but keeping his eyes on God Moses took his life and look forward and press on. Moses light was faith in God. There were so many things that seem impossible but with love for his faith that things of his past weren't impossible. What seemed like a disability or handicap disappeared within time. You can only imagine leaving so many people so far away from their home they knew faith and the love of God is real. How destructive that could've seem for Moses. For me coming home to a house not designed for me at that time, and Learning how to cook without hurting myself in the process. And before long, cleaning my house was becoming easier. The loneliness made the darkness even darker. It is also written that if a man is married let him stay married and please God him and his wife. But if a man is single let him stay single and please God and if you choose to be married in time he will find a wife if this with his heart desired. It is best that a man learning how to please God first and God will give him his heart desire. I agree with that because if a man knows how to please God he will make a great husband. When two people get together they both individually should know how to please God and have God in their life. There is a theory 1x1 equal one and if both people are whole then you have two whole people coming together as one but if there not whole you will have one half times a whole 1x1/2 equal half. So being single can be lonely at times but knowing that I would have someone in my life that is holy Jesus as myself then we wish you a great future in Jesus. I feel that would be a very promising and fulfilling life for both. Being lonely today only means tomorrow I will be fulfilled in a life in eternity. Besides focusing my life in Christ, brings me a peaceful spirit. Even when things may be hard, having peace in my life brings light to my situation. Surviving a darkroom can seem impossible without peace in your life. If you were to imagine yourself in a darkroom you need peace and focus and light with determination to see yourself through your situation. I do not have peace about my situation when I was in the hospital because all you can think about were the lights and monitors all around you and all you see day in and day out for doctors. Imagine a runner running a long race if he tumbles and fall he would most likely sit on the sidelines and recover from his injuries and after recovering from his injuries he will begin the race where he left off and that runner consider think of himself in a dark position while in pain. After recovering from the fall he was in the focus and he will continue his race. You won't see that runner getting back in the race back in darkness but in light, but If that runner do not recognize his fall then he would not be facing the truth. So my stroke was real and I know that certain things had to be face in my life. So I recognize and deal with the truth and after recognizing my situation I see the light and I'm able to find peace and go on living. After recognizing my situation I don't let other people disparage me I just continue to run the race. It is very easy to be disabled when you're in a darkroom. If you allow yourself to be discourage, then surviving the dark can be almost impossible to overcome. If my mother was alive I know she will be very proud because she received things same way I do. There came a time while in the hospital I experience going into shock. When noticing my surroundings for the very first time I went to a calm status shock. I could not recognize my surroundings while in the recovering room after surgery. There is no better way to describe that moment. I can compare it to being in a dark surrounding with no way out. The only way I can describe that moment is to compare it to a dark room with no way out. Just like being in that situation I had to take a long inhale and exhale to regain my mental strength to understand my situation. Being in unfamiliar situation in life is best described as a dark room with no way out. There also there were times while recovering I really felt that if I was to leave my bed and walk around the hospital there would be no way of find my way back. But taking the time to understand what was going on helped me regain my senses to figure my way out of that darkroom that I was in. So taking a long slow inhale then a slow long exhale gave me time to realize that there really is light in that dark situation. If there is anyone with any kind of illness that may make them feel trapped it is no different from being in a four cornered dark room. It really helps to see and to be around other people with similar experiences. When you feel you're not alone trying to survive in a darkroom in your life, it can ease the fear. It is very hard to find people family or friends who may understand what you're going through. If you picture yourself in a room with no way out you may feel the same way. Then to add to the situation and that room is dark that brings on confusion and you may feel that is no way out. Weeks and months went by before I became comparable about what has happened to me. That is why having God in my life took away the fear that came with surviving the moments.

Chapter 9

Confusion and mental pain can be destructive

In the holy Bible, there was a guy named Paul. Paul was out to persecute or kill any a preacher will follow preaches the name of Jesus Christ until one day in his travels while all alone he heard a voice that asked why do you hate me so much, it was the voice of Jesus Christ. At that moment Paul was blinded and cannot see. You can imagine confusion Paul had felt at that moment but the Lord son Paul to one of his followers to pray for that help him. After all the killing Paul has done to people who preach in the name of Jesus Christ that had to be very confusing not being able to see in front you. But Paul was bless to see again that he went on to believe in the name of Jesus Christ. You can see how nothings final when it comes to Jesus

Christ in anyone's life. Even though I had a stroke and I woke up after surgery half paralyze, not being able to move my left side of my body I was very confused. Having a foundation of prayer in my life had people praying for me I was blessed to be able to regain movements on my left side again. I'm a believer in the name of Jesus Christ the son of God. I was very confused very hurt, I was a wreck. At times I did not know what I would do. I do not know how to deal with my situation. It was one of my worst dreams. I have heard stories before my stroke of people who were in accidents and became fully paralyze and it took a very huge toll on their life. But then I also met and seen people who were wheelchairs and could not move his legs because of a spinal cord accident. I used to say to myself if I ever had to go through what they're going through I will prefer to not be limited all. But I could not been so wrong. You live and you learn. While in the hospital I have met a young lady by the name of Maria. Maria was only 22 years old she was in my physical therapy classes while talking to her I asked her what happened to her what put her in her position of not being able to walk and she told me one day she was sitting on her porch which was on the fifth floor of her building and she sat back on her foldaway chair and it was too close to the rail and she tipped over the rail and landed on the way to the concrete ground flat on her back and injured her spinal cord. In the conversation she also told me that the best thing her life was dancing and she can dance no more. And then there was a guy

Joseph, Joseph used to work on roofs until one day he fell off one and he landed straight down on his feet and shattered both of his legs and he could not walk because of injuries. When the day comes around and surprisingly changes your way of living because of an injury. Or something going on that could be very emotional or hard deal with and shatter your dreams and change your life be very confused and emotionally destroy if you're not blessed, very destructive to yourself and people around. I'm so glad I was blessed because never did I thought about taking my own life or hurting people around me. Even today, hurting myself is the last thing on my mind. I'm feeling very optimistic, I'm fighting my way back to 100%. It's Is hard enough and besides I have faith in God and believe in his son Jesus Christ and accepted him as my Savior I have eternal life. Suicide is a sin and if you allow yourself to go in that direction when you die and go to hell for eternity. To protect my spirit sometimes I would confess my love to Jesus twice maybe three times a day that's how much I love Jesus and want to be in heaven when I die. I will pray and say, thank you Lord Jesus for forgiveness for my sins and dying on the cross for me. I believe you are the son of God and you died on the cross for my sins and rose on the third day. Use the Lord in every way you want for your purpose on earth. When I was a regular church member before my stroke, whenever we held a baptism I will gladly and without hesitation did baptize every time. Not because I had to but dying to this world and the sins of my path and coming up the water and feeling cleansed made me feel so complete. I had the opportunity right now I will do it again. It doesn't matter about your church background or how long you were believer of Christ, you could turn your life over any time anywhere no matter what your past may have been like. The Lord will forgive your sins no matter what it was the Lord is very forgiving all you have to do is ask forgiveness as yours just for the asking. But before you come to the Lord and ask for forgiveness you should always forgive others as well. I found it very hard but with practice because very easy to have a heart like Jesus Christ. Jesus Christ came to this world to die for, he did not come to this world to be a part of this world or to condemn this world. Jesus Christ came to this world to be in the sacrifice for our sins. Jesus Christ came to this world to be the Lamb of God and to help us. He wants to make it possible for us to avoid hell and to have everlasting life. When I accepted Jesus in my life my life was changed. I repent for my sins and sin no more it was impossible to do it on my own. But with the help of our father it became very possible. There's only two roads in life and take, the road to heaven or rose hell, and I choose heaven and repent of my sins. Often times, we don't understand the things in life that God is still in control. That is why my heart is filled with peace and joy beyond understanding and it enables me to go through my struggles in life and that struggle is surviving the dark room like the stroke that I experience.

Chapter 10

I developing discipline in keeping your head above water

Three years before my stroke, I was a single man living alone. The church I attend will occasionally go on a conference to see other speakers or to strengthen our spirit in the Lord. This one particular conference was a three-day event in upstate New York. It was a bonfire for men only. We will get up in the morning have something to eat and pray and on the final day we will have a bonfire where we would receive a nail just like the nail that was used in the crucifixion of Christ, and we would spend hours in prayer and afterwards we will all separate and gone the words and have the intimate conversation with the Lord. It was such experience that everyone felt the anointing spirit of God had to hunger more of Jesus in our life. After that conference we had a wonderful night of sleep before returning back to the city. That trip was so uplifting to our spirit. It was like the living water the Lord speak of in the Bible. Jesus had approach a woman that was taking water from the well. And Jesus began to talk to her. As they talk, Jesus offered her water that will keep her from being in need of water ever again in fact she will not be thirsty, he was speaking of the Holy Spirit. As they continued to talk, she listened to every word that Jesus had to say. She could tell that Jesus was not the average person. The Holy Spirit lives with us every day of our lives because of his death we were blessed because of his death to be able to receive that living water in our lives today. That living water is what I experience in that conference. Soon it was Wednesday and it was church that evening I needed to shave my head because at that time I used to wear shave hairstyle, no hair on the top of my head so by the time I came home I needed to shave badly but I didn't because it was late. After Wednesday night church service, I felt so loved by God that after worshiping and continuing my communication with the Holy Spirit, I felt that there's got to be some way to show my love in a more definite way, while in my car getting ready to go home tears came to the corner of my eyes and while praying I made a promise to Lord that I love him so much that from this day forward I was not going to cut for a razor to my hair until I feel or hear a message from him to do so. After a while as my hair started to grow it became unmanageable so for months I did everything I can to make it presentable for church every Sunday morning. At first beginning, I was picking style after style. One day I decided that there were any styles left choose so remembering my promise to the Lord that Wednesday night I allow my hair to grow into dreads. I was very determined to keep my promise and not put a razor to my hair. Every Saturday I will sit on my porch and I would twist my hair to become presentable to wear to church on Sunday morning. Even though I worked 40 hours a week I will still be twisting my hair every Saturday. Before long the dreads in my hair were beginning to grow longer than I imagine. My dreads were longer than the average young lady hair but I was determined to keep my promise to God. Every time I look at my hair it made me feel warm knowing that it's only there because my love for God keeps growing. Some people will pay hundreds of dollars to have hair like mine but I knew why I had that kind hair and it was worth it. My dreadlocks were about 7 inches long evenly around my whole head and I took lots of pride in my dreadlocks. I have learned a lot of discipline, doing what I've done because to keep my hair in such a position for so long to a lot of discipline. While people were doing other good things like playing hanging out I will be home twisting my hair, sacrificing for the Lord meant a lot to me it also was teaching me at the same time. I felt the need to tell the world about his love so I started to give prayer service at my job. People did not agree to my methods but I did not let that stop me. Even though every area I found I was removed because of safety reasons at that time I worked in a warehouse for Xerox. A safety representative came to me at one of my studies, and told me that I had to leave. That made me so upset and depressed because I felt that I was doing the Lord's will and I'm determined to carry it out. As long as I was doing what the Lord wanted me to do it didn't matter. I was going to keep trying and today was no answer. One time I had no area for prayer service. And being that I had a job writing a forklift truck I would actually have a fan and a table on a skid and every time I gave prayer service I would actually get him a forklift truck get the skid and have prayer service. A lot of people couldn't understand why will go through so much but I learned not to pay it any attention because I knew what I was doing with the right thing to do not only that that's what the Lord wanted me to do. The Lord said, we as believers are the salt of the earth and we impact the people around us. Sometimes being a believer, we think that we cannot impact some people life. But I come to find out that it doesn't matter what you have where you been all which you know. Sometimes it's just being there and being a testimony to the fact that he is there and he will guide you out of your darkroom of your life. It can be the character or maybe just a conversation. Somehow is an impact on someone around us. We all have an obligation in life. Jesus even said so in a passage in the holy Bible. In the fifth chapter of Matthew 13 to 16 you are the salt of the earth but if the salt loses its flavor? Can you make it salty again? It would be thrown out and trampled underfoot as worthless you are the light of the world like a city on a hilltop cannot be hidden no one lights a lamp and then put it under a basket. Instead, a lamp is placed nice man, where it gives light to everyone in the house. In the same way that your good deeds shine out for all to see, so that everyone will praise your heavenly father. And it was our heavenly father that allow my life to continue on this earth to surgery, and the sweat of my physical therapy and effort than I'm allowed to put forth to go forward. Everyone has that same help from our heavenly father. In the past, I allow myself to have a free spirit and to do things that may have made me happy will make others happy so I could fit in. A lot of the actions wasn't not God's way. But I've learned, when we let Satan influence our lives, we causes certain things to be activated in our lives. So being that some of the things that I've done was carnal and not God's way I just opened the door for Satan to work in my life. And that was a big lesson learned in the holy Bible and book of Galatians 6:8 for he that soweth to his flesh shall of the flesh reap corruption ; but he that soweth to the spirit shall of the spirit reap new everlasting. Or to put it another way Lasciviousness, or lack of resistance or control, over one's life is a tool used by Satan to distract believers and take their focus off God's words. When you cater to your flesh and give into selfish, carnal desires, you position yourself to experience the consequences of your behavior. Man is a spirit, Who possesses a soul (the place where your mind, will, and emotions reside), **of which are housed in a body. God did not design the body to be in control of everything instead, he intended for you to develop your spirit man so that it will operate in the lines of his word, enabling you to live a life that is rich and blessings.** I may be out shopping going about my everyday activities but knowing that I have Jesus in my life my dark rooms are very bearable and possible. Lust of the eyes is a sin. Sometimes we all can have that problem and don't even realize it when it happens. It don't have to be over a woman, but it can be over things that you buy a new should because of your economic situation lusting over certain things will Drag you to buying things you don't need. There is a worldly saying that a lot of people don't realize they would say the love of money is a sin. But that's wrong, it is the lust of money is a sin. That's why praising God is very useful in my life and he will be that important to anyone in a darkroom. Jesus Christ followers, is the salt and the light of this world and it is our responsibility to let our light shine to impact the people around us. My struggles in my life and praising Jesus and knowing that he's always there to help me out my dark situations are seen by others. Being a light and I saw of this world always It was turn out to be very successful for the Lord because my effort and belief in Jesus is going to steer a lot of people to Lord Christ Jesus and by being salt and light of this world will help others in lives. I've came a long way from the day of going to a church conference. It also is forming me for today. Living a life and being disabled takes a lot of discipline. Whenever you have to live a life in the dark to survive you must become discipline in many ways. I've seen so many people disabled and had to learn how to do things so differently in their life. A lot of things I never took note of before I had my stroke. But disabled people have a lot of courage and a lot of fight to go forward. One of the biggest challenge I faced was forgiveness. Lots of people do not mean any harm but they tend not to think about things as fast as we would like for them to. A person that's not able to move quickly enough for some people, tends to make them upset to the point that they would disregard did disablement and move around them very quickly. So if person is disabled or maybe even handicap have to forgive their motions and keep trying to put their best effort in front of them, and keep going. In the book of Matthew's 6:14 for if you forgive men their trespasses your heavenly father will also forgive you Through all the praying I have done from the day of the conference the Lord was also grooming me for today having a life being disabled Lord knows everything before it happens. The Lord knows the ending before the beginning in everyone's life and his love stretches further than the East to the West. So I've learned you should never worry if the Lord knows your problem that you're facing because he does any years all prayers. Sometimes you may think that he don't hear you when he does. Just because you don't get an answer right after you pray doesn't mean that he did I hear you. Most of the time he's already working on the answer to your prayers before you pray. If the person was a darkroom is easy to get discouraged you don't see your way out as clearly as you would like to but in time thanks changes answers would become before you and sometimes all it takes is patience and waiting on the Lord for your prayers to be answered before your eyes. Sometimes it can become a miracle right before your eyes. I did a lot of praying from the day I was in recovery today I came home from the hospital but the Lord has reason for everything that goes on in your life. You might not understand but you must trust and have faith in the Lord because the Lord did not make any mistakes I have encourage many people in my position today. Not realizing it I was the answer to a lot of people prayers and didn't know it. I've asked the Lord to use me for his purpose and in a lot of ways I am being use and its purpose to encourage and to help others understand and give hope to a lot of people who are living in a darkroom in their life. Another Way, God has taught me discipline was being on the Dean's list in college and working 52 hours a week at my job. And with church being on the AV team serving in a ministry going to college full-time and working full-time while at work I also was a medic and hold prayer service in the warehouse. Discipline is very important to surviving the dark rooms of your life. It was the Lord Jesus Christ they gave me life and a life to live with the reason. Living in a darkroom can make you so discourage that you see no way out or around your problems but is very important to keep your head above water and believe in yourself and know without a doubt that God did not make a mistake when it comes down to who and what you are in the world today. When I look back my in my life I can see how hard it was for my mother because she lived in a darkroom for a many moments in her life I've seen it firsthand. I was also blessed see others survive the dark rooms in their life. Keeping ahead to the sky can sometimes be harder than just words. But if by chance you're able to do that then you only have great things to look forward to. Imagine yourself leaving a darkroom after being in a darkroom for a long time. It is so refreshing to breathe. The heartbeat even changes and you feel so relaxed that is the same way you feel leaving a situation that may pressure you and make you seem disabled. To stay alive and being positive about my future, it comes down to having a intimate relationship with the Holy Spirit. For example, if you were married and your spouse was changing clothes in the bedroom, having a intimate relationship means that you could go in the bedroom and have a conversation with your spouse. You will cause that an intimate moment with a relationship and conversation. With Christ Jesus, that's the kind of relationship you would like to develop with him. Whenever I'm down and I don't know the answers I have a place in my house that I will consider very holy where if I'm very upset, or bothered, I can go to that spot and I can have that intimate conversation with the Holy Spirit. And with faith I know beyond a shadow of a doubt that the Lord Jesus is my prayer and conversation. I just be careful that other people don't see me praying at times I don't think they will understand. Not that I'm embarrassed, it's just that it's private, it's a relationship between me and God. It's very intimate, because I can tell my Lord anything. It doesn't matter if anyone seem you're not, it's just intimate. God desires to have a intimate relationship with you, And to produce his life to us, rather it's the wrong kind of life, or the right kind of life, he won us to do the same. God's purpose in life is to reveal himself in our lives, and through our lives. And it's the highest priority. In order for that to happen he must reveal himself to you. Having a intimate relationship with God goes further than what you can see, touch or feel. It is the will of God to have a intimate relationship with us. Being saved is not enough. For example of a intimate relationship with God in the holy Bible David had a true intimate relationship with God. Psalms 63: 1-8 reads, oh God, you are my God ; I earnestly reach for you. My soul thirsts for you; my whole body longs for you in this parched and weary land where there is no water. I have seen you in your sanctuary and glaze upon your power and glory. Your unfailing love is better than life itself ; how I praise you, I will praise you as long as I live, lifting up my hands to your prayers. You satisfied me more than the riches feast. I will praise you with songs of joy. I lie awake thinking of you, meditate and on you through the night. Because you are my help her, I seem for joy and the shadows of your wings. Can you say that you have a relationship with God? More than any place person or thing. Having a intimate relationship with God means my soul hungers after God. Everyone has a direct relationship with that. He is the creator of this world, he is the creator of this world, the sustainer, the ruler of this world. Some people feel that they're so far away from God they feel very distant from God but they know they got it creator God is what keeps them. They may go to church, read the Bible from time to time and may even pray. But they don't understand, that God hears them. It is a story that I used to tell some believers in my prayer class, and goes a little like this, say there were three kids living in the household would one mother, the mother is cooking dinner, and one of the kids decided to go in the kitchen and bother their mother, more likely by pulling on her skirt telling her repeatedly they want to eat right now, and the mother keep replying, dinner be done in a minute. But the kid do not understand that the mother has many responsibilities at the same time. It's not that the mother did not hear the child, but the mother is keeping the child at the same time of taking care of her responsibilities. And after all said and done, you can see the love that the mother has for the child. God has the same kind of love for us. I can consider myself a child of God and God is the mother, and I'm repeating the asking for attention. But God loving me as much as he do has patients and never forgot about me, that's why I love the Lord. It's very important that when we experience the dark rooms of our lives, we experience the love of God also. It is the

Marvin McKelvey

love of Jesus Christ that sustained me and kept me from drowning keeping my head above water. I'm a survivor of my stroke. It's not over till it's over praises be to God our heavenly father.